The Queue
(Poetry: The Cenotaph Collections)

'*Testicles Without Penis*'
(A Series)

Blac Rebondzeh

Miraclaire Publishing
Kansas City/Yaounde

MIRACLAIRE PUBLISHING LLC
Kansas City, (MO) USA

Website: *www.miraclairepublishing.com*
Email: *info@miraclairepublishing.com*

P.O. Box 8616
Yaounde, Cameroon

ISBN-13: 978-0615997186
ISBN-10: 061599718X

All rights reserved.
No part of this publication may be reproduced by any means, graphic, electronic, or mechanical, including photocopying, recording, taping or by any information storage retrieval system without the prior written permission of the copyright holder, except in the case of brief quotations embodied in critical articles and reviews.

© 2014 Miraclaire Publishing
Blac Rebondzeh

Printed in the United States of America

Miraclaire Publishing makes every effort to ensure the accuracy of all the information ("Content") in its publications. However, Miraclaire and its agents and licensors make no representations or warranties whatsoever as to the accuracy, completeness, or suitability for any purpose of the Content and disclaim all such representations and warranties, whether expressed or implied to the maximum extent permitted by law. Any views expressed in this publication are the views of the author and are not necessarily the views of Miraclaire.

Dedication

To the everlasting memories of Mom

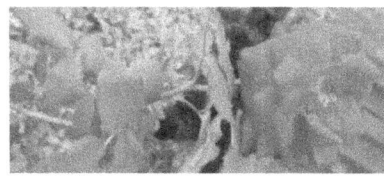

Ten years
And still
The eyes of tears
To heal.

When all is gone,
Then all's been done.

Acknowledgments

I have met and interacted with wonderful individuals over the course of time, whose lives, words, actions and teachings have been a veritable source of inspiration to me as a poet. These include my very first and lifetime teachers Julie Shiri, and Martin Mokom (the story teller); my teachers at secondary and high school, including especially Alex Ngati, Prodencia Ngong, Samuel Ngorang, Sammy Arembi, and Jude Mfah, from 1985 to 1993; my literature professors at the University Rosaline Jua, Charles Nama, Abraham Tala, and George Nyamndi, from 1993 to 1996 (but George Nyamndi till date); my program coordinators on the Cameroon Radio and Television (CRTV) Bamenda *Literary Workshop* A. T. Menget and P. S. Romanus, from 1986 to 1992; and finally a host of friends, including most especially Doris Litzinger, Kathleen Wit, Rosemary Nsiaga, Gregory Nkepang, Tikum M. Azonga, and Azore Opio.

The photo of the traditional Bantu Grassfields armchair with power symbolism was obtained with the kind assistance of Victor Taku.

& & & & &

The title of this series, '**Testicles without penis**' which is not to be read literally, originates as a Bantu proverb of *Mbo'-Widikum*, '***Mbin-mbin, tsey kirt***', figuratively read to mean '**An enclave of gold.**'

PREFACE

The queue is the beginning volume in a series of poetry collections under the general title, *'Testicles without penis'*. This intriguing and thought provoking title simply paraphrases as *potentials without a way out* or *an enclave of gold*, and therefore professes the paradox in the human experience. The title itself is an African (Bantu) proverb from the Widikum tribe in the North Western Region of Cameroon. It is a metaphor used here to paint the picture of the human situation embellished with the fullness of potentials, vigour, high spirit, and all the human and natural resources that go to guarantee the wellbeing and prosperity of human life on earth, all of which ironically and embarrassingly collide with an unfortunate lack, not only of the means, but also of the will to take full advantage of them, as a result of the selfishness of man himself. Think of a certain fertile arable enclave of land in the equatorial rain forest; it is without a road leading in and out of it, and the native peasant farmers will have all the best farm produce, but their lives would never see a change, as long as there is no way to take their produce out to the market, and as long as policy makers don't see the need for a farm to market road. Think of a union of cocoa and coffee farmers who have enormous potentials to build a large fortune and earn a decent living; the lack of good leadership takes them to nowhere, as there won't be a proper and honest bargain for them to make a fair income in accordance with their labour input. Think of yourself as a High School graduate with very good grades and full potentials to do well at the University and make a good career in not a distant future, but you are a downcast and in earnest lack the means and sponsorship to earn that University education. Think of a certain country (or in fact, a world) full of all the natural and human resources that one can think of; without (the right) leadership, the good fortune amounts to nothing. The lack of a farm-to-market road, for instance, is to a certain farmer with all the best produce, as is the lack of a means to an end to any capable person with full potentials, that is, the lack of anything that can be used to take advantage of any given potential or good fortune.

The poems of *The queue* and those of subsequent volumes in the series *'Testicles without penis'* are therefore written against the mindset that the world is full of every good thing one can imagine BUT for a proper means and/or will by which to take full advantage. Thus, the poem that lends its name to the series – a limerick – opens this volume (and will the subsequent ones) by vividly illustrating the proverb to the reader. This is done with the help of an agile bird of prey which has command, both of the sky from where it lurks on its powerful wings to scan and scale its preys, and of the earth which provides hideouts – little bushes, shrubs and trees – from where to ambush the preys, but whose force and agility would come down to nothing if it lacks the appropriate claws to cling onto a chosen prey and take full control of it. The collections in the series are designed to be a cenotaph. The series is therefore built in honour and memory of the poet's mother and best friend, Julie, who demonstrated the force and the will to create the means by which to take advantage of the world's good fortune, but who left the 'scene of action' so early in her prime – much sooner than was expected. In this respect, a eulogy for her – the epilogue, *A letter to Mom* is placed on the inside back cover of this volume (as will be on the subsequent ones).

The title of the present volume, *The queue* is itself the title of a short poem – one of the early poems in it, which in a way, professes the sense of organization and discipline to be enjoyed in the poet's homeland. The reader is actually led into the volume by yet another short poem, titled *Prelude*, subtitled *Your cup of tea*, a poem that paints life as 'turn taking'. Thus, in preparing the reader's mind to explore the content of *The queue*, the former is reminded that life is all about turn taking and should be so, and that all of mankind, irrespective of nationality, age, race, social class, learning, profession, and financial standing begins in one and the same dramatic but humble fashion – conception, gestation, and birth, and ends in one and the same dramatic but humble fashion – death and mortal breakdown, and that whatever happens in between depends on each individual's search and choice of THE most appropriate traffic lane to tread through life.

Life, as one can imagine, is a traffic lane full of obstacles which mankind is literally called upon to tread, and of course, without obstacles, life could be a smooth, straight road into the wilderness, full of vagueness and emptiness. The joint abundance of obstacles and the abundance of means of surmounting such obstacles is what creates excitement and the joint force and will to carry on with life, the life which, in turn, gently creates the joint fulfilment and quest for the final rest that creeps in towards the end of it. On the contrary, the joint abundance of obstacles and the embarrassing lack of the means of surmounting them is what dampens the human soul and spirit and subdues the force to carry on with life and the fulfilment that should creep in towards the end of it. Coming into life and facing these life's obstacles to either surmount them or be surmounted by them is like joining a queue and taking a turn to either get it right or get it wrong. In this queue of life, some naturally find themselves in the front and others in the back, the latter with no guarantee to ever reach the front and the former with equally no guarantee to forever remain at the front. In a paradox, while some people may negotiate their positions either in the middle or in front of the queue, others may simply break the queue when and wherever it pleases them, thus pushing others, deserving or non-deserving, steps backward.

In exploring the content of *The queue*, the reader is therefore expected to find the complex paradox of human life in queuing up and taking turns, albeit in ways, melodies, tones, patterns, and settings that are as widely diversified and varied as are the poems themselves.

FOREWORD

I have searched the landscape of Cameroonian Anglophone poetry many years now, and have seen but precious little to enchant my senses. Here finally is one collection that sits me down; one collection that rewards me with a sense of having got there! I can finally say *here* is something to talk about, something to show off.

Either fired by misjudgment or trapped by effacement, Blac Rebondzeh says of the noble art of poetry that it is 'soft a thing to grapple with' "At the steering wheel". Nothing could be more inimical to the truth. Poetry is a difficult art to manipulate. The fact that it comes relatively easy to a (chosen) few does not take away from its demands. Poetry does not countenance neophytic adventures. And this collection is crystal proof that the warning is heeded. The hand is steady, the tone à propos, the matter arresting. We are here in a veritable green field of imaginative production.

The collection comprises 47 poems (if one excludes the epilogue *A letter to Mom*), clustered into the *Prelude* (5 poems), *The queue* (9 poems), *Night* (9 poems), *Siphonaptera* (6 poems), *Curse* (7 poems), *The woodpecker* (8 poems), and *Dilapidation* (3 poems). *The queue*, a six-line acronymic puzzle, also lends is title to the collection, so that one is compelled to look closely at it (the six-line poem) for clues to the collection's overall direction and emphasis. And when one does, one is immediately confronted with metaphors of pre-eminence:

> In Yaounde, there is a queue,
> And whenever you find the queue,
> The U's and E's always queue up
> Behind the Q, U-E, U-E,

> U at all times leading the E,
> And Q is always at the top.

Whether one can decipher the puzzle matters little, especially if we view it as symbolic. What is important, on the contrary, is the fact that some letters fall behind others, some lead at all times, and yet others are forever at the top. One can substitute these letters with such paradigms of context as race, technology, the economy, culture, religion, gender, etc. The temper of the collection can thus be seen to be sustained by concerns of intercourse, natures of interaction. It is in this spirit that "Your cup of tea", the signal poem of the *Prelude*, cautions: 'As the zeal for us to be, You cook your own cup of tea.' 'And drink it', we are almost tempted to add. No divine ordering here, only human responsibility. This much the eagle tells the gull in the little animal fable, "The gull and the eagle":

> Let me put it in black on white:
> ...
> Be razor-sharp – with full rigour!
> Without this fit, you can't make it
> In this sea home full of sardines,
> But nev'r enough for ev'ryone.

The poetic intentions here is not only constative in the sense that it foregrounds the status quo (some lead and others are led); it is also prospective since it provides exit routes out of the status quo; (to make it, in other words, to lead instead of being led, one has to be sharp, razor-sharp). In a context in which nature's generosity, 'this sea home full of sardines', is subverted by human greed, one must indeed be razor-sharp to survive. In this context, even fathers have negated their mission: 'My father is a wicked blood thirsty monster', laments the voice in "My father's arsenal: A note to Azonga", provoking the echo:

> O winds of change that blow across,
> I cannot wait to be at home!
> When shall you travel to the South
> For me to be at home at last?
> "Winds of change" (2008).

The naïve manna-from-the-West attitude inherent in this yearning has been at the heart of African's undoing. There is no free lunch, anywhere, as "Siphonaptera: A letter to Dad" cautions: 'They cannot help us, But they take all that is ours'; no benevolent winds, either from the West or from any other where else: 'They are vampires/With legs to leap and stick' "Siphonaptera". We may miss the meaning of this neologism; we would certainly not miss the suggestiveness of its beginning syllables. You cook your own lunch or starve; you raise your own winds or perish – that's the bottom line!

The lead poem, "Hitting a country rock" provides responses to all the interrogations raised in the other minor poems. "Hitting a country rock" is an ambitious piece both in its length and its sweep. Bucolic and epic at the same time, it brings together with startling ease, Wordswordian pastoralism, or shall we say romanticism, and African lyricism reminiscent of Okot p'Bitek in "Song of Lawino" and "Song of Ocol". The poem is actually a saga of the British Southern Cameroon's trajectory, from its trusteeship plenty to its post-independence leanness, a leanness ushered in 'one dry season early in the eighties'. We think here immediately of the presidential decree of 1984 that changed the country's name from United Republic to the Republic quite simply, thus making nonsense of the country's recent history. Result?

> With ever scanty broods and shrinking bulbs,
> The happy valley life was bound to leave,
> And, since, it's been so hard for dependants,

That giving up is all the weak can do
But not all give up. The victims are in three categories: 'The folks who scan the bins and talk alone', 'The folks who can't take it and so take off', and 'The folks who brace to fight the obstacle'. This last category encapsulates the hope of regeneration, driven as they are by the rhetorical question:

> So couldn't they simply drill right through the stone
> And let the pear tree tap root fire right on,
> To let the whole valley rejoice again,
> To see the fruits return in their numbers
> To rejuvenated arms and fingers
> To lead us to the good old days again?

Hope is not lost because not all have given up. "Hitting a country rock" is an allegorical hurrah! to peoples in varying situations across the world; people who refuse to succumb to adversity; people who believe in the transience of trial and the permanence of felicity. It echoes, in a most befitting way, the final message of this endearing collection, and does so with the kind of beauty mirrored in every single verse of the collection.

George D. Nyamndi, PhD Literature
Vice-Dean/Admissions and Records, Faculty of Arts
University of Buea, Buea, Cameroon

Contents

Dedication
Acknowledgements
PREFACE i
FOREWORD v

PRELUDE
(1) Prelude: Your cup of tea 3
(2) The pick 4
(3) The naked hungry son 5
(4) The riddle 6
(5) Old boys in the blues 7

THE QUEUE
(6) The queue 11
(7) Song of an old nanny 12
(8) A shoal of fertile oily salmons 13
(9) Hitting a country rock 14
(10) November 6th 2012 20
(11) The gull and the eagle 21
(12) Rising at dawn 22
(13) Ladybug 23
(14) My father's arsenal: A note to Azonga 24

NIGHT
(15) Last night 27
(16) Winds of change 28
(17) Amid the heat of fated flights 29
(18) Along the river of Jordan 31
(19) The black star 34
(20) The brown pear leaf 35
(21) The tern 36
(22) This can't be true; this can't be true; I can't believe! ... 37
(23) The silly arse licker 38

SIPHONAPTERA
(24) Siphonaptera: A letter to Dad 41
(25) Children in bondage 43
(26) Let's no more leave the riverside 44
(27) I won't accept a sit on top 45
(29) Green bananas won't stay green 49

CURSE
(30) Curse 53
(31) Speak with me! 54
(33) Leftward movement 56
(34) The express mail 57
(35) At the steering wheel 58
(36) Tolerance 59

THE WOODPECKER
(37) The woodpecker 63
(38) Power 64
(39) The saga of Sandra Laing 65
(40) Come-no-go 66
(41) And I fear not 67
(43) The rhythm of my heart 69
(44) O Michael! 70

DILAPIDATION
(46) We humble through the humble gates 74
(47) Rest: The peace at crest 75

A Letter to Mom 77

PRELUDE

Testicles without penis

I've the blue with my wings
And the green with the lings,
But I'm zero
If I'm mellow,
But I have not the clings.
            (2008)

(1) Prelude: Your cup of tea

As the bright radiance comes on,
You commence as we have done;
As she goes way down the loo,
You round up as we all do;
As the zeal for us to be,
You cook your own cup of tea.
                             (2007)

(2) The pick

There comes Demise
Lurking above the healthy chicks,
And like a dice,
He falls upon …, and duly picks.
(2003)

(3) The naked hungry son

I won't watch the TV
Any longer, even for fun,
Until the naked hungry son
Of the North finds envy.
                    (2012)

(4) The riddle

As I trod all along the wobbling trails
And witty landscapes of a periled time,
A muddy story glided down the rails
And dully softly placed me on a dime:
'The world is like a gorgeous butterfly.'
And so, I stopped and turned to have a say,
But found not any butterflies that fly,
For there was fog that blanketed my way,
And I was blind to all that lay in it.
As I picked up the pace and tried to flee,
I heard, again, a firm but calmer wit
That, gentle though, avowed the simile:
    'It's either like a flashy beam that looms,
    Or foxtail lily bearing brittle blooms.'

(2007)

(5) Old boys in the blues

Here we are, O good friends,
Great minds at the drawing boards
And colleagues of the 2000 force,
All, still old boys in the blues!
It's since been the same,
If only not now worse,
And we have been in the blues!
I cannot help but ask myself:
When shan't we take soft loans,
And stop to cash ahead of time,
But let our pouches remain stuffed
And leave our assets get mature
Till dawn of each new month?

When shall we, for once, be so prepared
To lead the lineage out to enchantment,
Oftentimes, dinner away from the abode,
Customary rides down to the beach,
And vacation trips, off to Waza
For copious awareness of the homeland
And kids' fruition with the spices of life?

For how much more time ahead
Do we have to hang about and wait
For such a point in time to come?
Or, do we enjoy oblivion?

O!
Old boys in the blues,
When shall we not be blue?

(2007)

THE QUEUE

(6) The queue

In Yaounde, there is a queue,
And whenever you find the queue,
The U's and E's always queue up
Behind the Q, U-E, U-E,
U at all times leading the E,
And Q is always at the top.
(2010)

(7) Song of an old nanny

My poor little darling,
I'd been brought in last night
In anticipation
Of your privileged birth
Here, where the time is still,
And I have not my life.

Today, my love's no more
For you and your siblings,
But your own progeny
To whom I'm not nanny:
They see their mom in me.
How I wish I'd borne them!

Tomorrow, I'm over
To their own progeny,
And that would be the life
That I'd led on the job.
I've grown to love it so,
Or else, where do I go?
                    (2009-2011)

(8) A shoal of fertile oily salmons

This house's not a herd of fat buffalos
Astride the lion prides of the Ngorongoro,
But a shoal of fertile oily salmons
Astride the keen bears from their winter slumber.
                    (2010-2011)

(9) Hitting a country rock

i
A yarn goes of an avocado tree
That history holds had known the good epoch,
But which, the last three decades, now gone by,
Have brought her down to endure a dire fate.

ii
A great man, in his sunny acumen,
And all his good and welcoming humour
Conjectures, nothing hurts a simple man
Who barely wants to be in his own days:

The early rising up upon the dawn
To see a brand new light of day come down,
And to the schedule of the silent night,
The schedule that would always seem routine –

The rising at the very first cock crow,
The rising at the cockerel's humble try,
The rising at the blackbird's cheerful songs,
The rising at the clock bird's even calls;

The rising to the sparrow's squirmy chirps,
The rising to the hen's edgy cackles,
The rising to the goats with quirky bleats,
The large bulls that bellow, and cows that low;

The rising up to start a usual day,
The rising up to serve domestic beasts,
The rising up to nosh the oxen fit,
The rising up to set the tasks amidst

    The songs that tell the fine people's hist'ry
And bring to roost the early childhood days,
    The songs that make tireless an arduous day
And make the grasses all to fall asleep;

    The fibre hat that shields the violent god,
The man who mans and trails the plough at work,
    The wit and wisdom that come on the job,
The man, the plough, the oxen that heaves on;

    The joy of exertion all day on-field,
The joy of seeding when the fields are set,
    The joy to have control on how they move,
The joy to see labour comes to fruition,

    The joy to pick the leaves and shake fruit trees,
Unearth peanuts, the yams and cassavas,
    And break the maize and bring bananas down,
And beat the beans, and see bounties head home

    With songs that tell the fine people's hist'ry,
The songs to whose rhythm the people dance,
    The songs that take away the pile of stress,
The songs with which the dying sun will set

    As we return to little cats that purr,
The ev'ning chores that lead us to dinner,
    Bed-time stories, and bed-time ties and bonds
And seeding of the little boys and girls;

    But night-time stresses do not stay away:
From stress of work, the hooting of the owls,
    The good suggestions of the dying night,
And how to wake up to a brand new day.

iii

But so many are men and women of
The time, and babies, children, and the youths
    Who've gone down, in the valley of plenty,
And these have truly been the good peoples.

    A reader finds a compass in a square,
A shape he severs into equal two
    From top right angle down to bottom left,
To find the tiny little paradise.

    As green as she had been in times gone by,
With firm and healthy hands on healthy arms,
    A body that would stand upright and firm –
A maiden in the midst of old women,

    The tree knew fresh shoots in colours of sorts;
Like no one else, she brightly bloomed all year,
    And bore her fruits in overlapping shifts
That kept the valley's hopes in life ahead.

    The hanging, healthy looking bulbs were fresh,
And fleshy; so oily a noble fruit,
    Of which we ate, to keep body and soul!
And from the sky, like from the earth, all ate:

    The bony skins and all the tribes on wings,
The go-on-four – the cat, mole, mouse, and dog;
    Our neighbours fed, and microbes took the
specks.
So all fed well, and all the land fared well.

You cannot find a people depressing
When birds that fly twitter and flap their wings,
    When fish that swim perform Olympic dives,
When all that be, great and little are seen:

    Palm oil from oil palms that litter the slopes,
The true envy of the orang-utan,
    The envy that would later spread so wide,
The envy that the valley pioneered;

    Pea oil from peanuts that linger about,
And all the oils that all the grains can serve;
    And all the waters from the mountain tops
That robe the slopes and build great water ways;

    The dust of gold and special rocks that sleep,
The boards of wood beneath the canopies,
    The milk of rubber that would hit the roads,
The roads that are not here, but over there,

    The wide valleys that hold the man-made lakes,
The falling waters with the tones of force,
    The pastures on the expands of grass fields,
The mountains, plains, and lowlands down to sea;

    The beaches and the sands in abundance,
The mouths of flows with fine-grained deposits,
    The mangrove juices in the mangrove fields,
The muscles and the wit of folks themselves.

              iv
    But all was going to change, and then it did:
One dry season early in the eighties,
    The pear tree tap root hit a country rock
That changed the course of hist'ry once for good,

      And after decades of amazing growth,
The nails began to drop right on our watch,
      The shrinking arms so clear for all to see,
And ripples so soon followed down the trunk.

      With ever scanty broods and shrinking bulbs,
The happy valley life was bound to leave,
      And, since, it's been so hard for dependants,
That giving up is all the weak can do,

      With three brands of those who hang on to life:
The folks who scan the bins and talk alone,
      The folks who can't take it, and so take off,
The folks who brace to fight the obstacle,

      The choice, until poetry time, having been
To dig and lift the country rock away,
      An option that has proved too expensive,
The evil rock so firm and poised to stay.

v

      If asked, I think they've bungled all the way,
For country rocks so massive cannot move
      When we do not yet buy the good wisdom
And fine technology that make them move.

      I do not find the giant excavator,
The kind that would pick out the three angles
      And lift the mighty rock and clear the way,
But I can see the mighty drills that drill.

      As problems come to men and not to trees,
We count our paces as we feel our thighs;
      To kill the owl that gnaws our tender hearts,
We do not have to stare his staring eyes;

    Some do, but one can't be so considerate
To take a drink from a poisoned chalice;
    So couldn't they simply drill right through the stone
And let the pear tree tap root fire right on,

    To let the whole valley rejoice again,
To see the fruits return in their numbers
    To rejuvenated arms and fingers
To lead us to the good old days again?

                                   (2007 - 2013)

(10) November 6th 2012

On this day of our Lord,
November sixth, Tuesday,
The sun has laid a trail
Across the Atlantic
From this Gulf of Guinea
To that of Mexico
In one revelation
Of two sides of herself:
At those western fringes,
The sun rises at dawn
And duly sets at dusk,
But she would rise at dawn
At these eastern fringes
And stay airborne for life
Despite the fork tail tern,
For impossible fads
Do not live at this end.
(2012)

(11) The gull and the eagle

Two birds of prey, Gull and Eagle,
Toil, each, to keep a home running;
At the Eagles', thriving is high,
And Gull sets out to find out how:

'Eagle, Eagle, what more is there
That you can do that I cannot?
Remember, we both have the sea.'
'You're right, dear Gull,' Eagle replied,
'But we serve in diff'rent sectors,
You know, and mine has lots more fish.
Old friend, you can't really compare.
Besides, I find the frail fair game,
Their youngsters being the easy picks…'
'But all of that, I'd long begun,'
Poor Gull broke in, desperately,
'And even check unguarded nests.'
'But that's not all,' Eagle pushed on.
'Let me put it in black on white;
I want to be honest with you.
To crown it up, I'm also sharp.
Be razor-sharp – with full rigour!
Without this fit, you can't make it
In this sea home full of sardines,
But nev'r enough for ev'ryone.'

Gull then nodded up to the sky,
And seemed to mumble, 'God willing,'
And turning swiftly homeward bound,
He left Eagle no further word.

      (2010-2013)

(12) Rising at dawn

Sometimes, somewhere,
When people rise at dawn
To find themselves in a strong pose,
They tend to find it very hard
To see that they had not been there
And so can let it go.
(2010)

(13) Ladybug

Amidst the storm of one infamous day,
The pale, white face of Ladybug
Was deeply tinted with pinkish patches
And bright, colourful, rainbow waves,
That looked so wearily gloomy, and drawn
Into the laps of a mountain
Of thick double metric ton of red wig,
Against an assorted background
Of friends from local and far away dens,
As Bug arrived in dense escort
That rode and flew, prepared to the letter,
To check the loaded sentry bees
To whom he owes his lasting primacy.
       (2011)

(14) My father's arsenal: A note to Azonga

My father is a wicked blood thirsty monster
Who has outlived his legitimate age,
And is now surviving on burgled time
By siphoning blood from every next-of-kin,
And not letting them ever see the light of day.
Well, some of his children still revere him;
Think of the exuberant red carpets
They are allowed to spread before him,
And the hailing merriments that greet his words
Right in the parlours of some neighbours
And distant commiserating households
Where they have, however, gone to seek refuge,
To escape the heat from the blazing roof
And the welcoming claws in his arsenal.
Though from behind, we should not pick up dew,
The path is still perilously dewy at this time.

(2010)

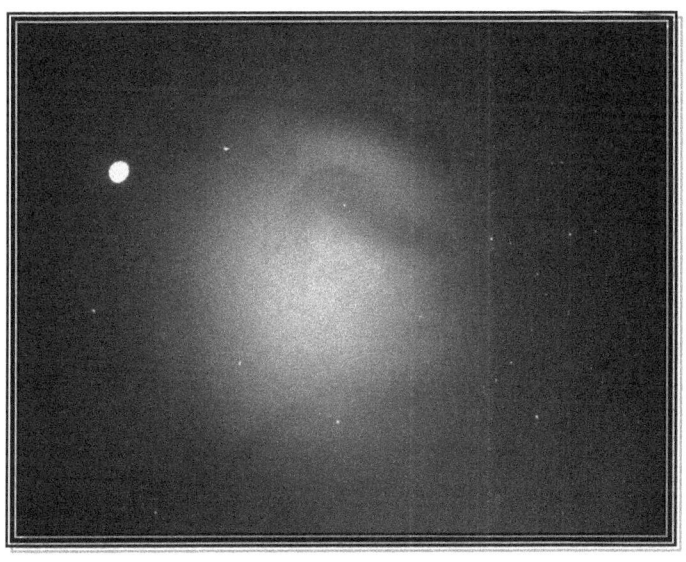

NIGHT

(15) Last night

Last night, a miniature mouse kept vigil
As I lay down to rest from a long day.
Scampering and squeaking at a corner,
The timid one woke me from my snooze.
So I got out of bed and lit the lamp
To see the extricating spectacle.
But then there came again, calm and quiet,
And the illusive mouse, I could not find.
A cockroach soon rushed in staring at me
As if to let me have the full account.
But as I got my ears widened for him,
He stopped and braced, and uttered not a word.
So I asked him why he had come at all,
But giving him no extra time to speak,
I lost my temper just right there and then,
And let the anger rush out like a stream
Before going to warm my cot again,
But fin'lly losing all my forty winks
To not only the fullness of the moon,
But also to the hooting of the owls.
Then all the night time stress notwithstanding,
The little nightjar came again to work,
Still scampering, but now crunching a meal.
'O poor thing of a little hungry fig.!'
I cried and tried to grab a dose again.
                              (2009)

(16) Winds of change

     South East Asia through New Europe,
The winds do blow, so let them blow.

     O winds of change that blow across,
I cannot wait to be at home!

     When shall you travel to the South
For me to be at home at last?
(2008)

(17) Amid the heat of fated flights

Amid the heat of fated flights,
The thumping of the liberties,
The testing of the will of men,
The will to live or not to live,
    Where all seemed well
    But well not safe,

There was a man of war who came
On stage and told the world at large:
'You are with us or not with us,
For what you do will speak for you
    Where all seems well
    But well not safe;

'What makes us differ from the imps,
The pack of senseless vampire bats –
Designers of the polished sculls
That gaze from mounts of naked bones,
    Where all seems well
    But well not safe,

'The wanton heads-of-goat that smirk
And feel the feelings not of men
And busy veins that all connect
To all our hearts, the hearts that beat
    When all seems well
    But well not safe;

'And us, right here, who lack the nerves,
The reckless nerves that charge and slay,
But full of zeal and will to keep
Their backs right down, their backs right down
    When all seems well
    But well not safe,

'Is that of night, the darkest night
Of all the nights, for them who slay;
And day, for us, the brightest day,
Who live and turn the wheel of life
    When all seems well
    But well not safe.'
                      (2010)

(18) Along the river of Jordan

Along the river of Jordan
Where multitudes had assembled,

A great many an age in flight
And many more to see the light;

But there will come the hereafter,
When time will halt and age will die.

A few are slaves, who came to us,
But kings have lived and more will be.

A lot are those of our brethren
Who seek the scepter of our Lord –

Generals who stand not their grounds,
In Mark's own authentication.

The Master and his men went on
Towards the town where he was born,

And as the twelve trailed Him in fear,
He then held up His cup to them:

'Behold we will soon reach the point
Before the scribes and the chief priests,

And there, a man will give me up
To earn the trophy of his life,

And I will face a penal end
To grace the hearts of non-Mormons.'

So, they will throw Him to the wolves,
That He should pay for His dissent;

And they will rag Him and curse Him,
Water Him down and strike Him down.

And then the mischievous schoolboys,
For they, ignorant Zebedees,

Cornered their master, so garbled
Behind the backs of their comrades:

'Grant us, Master, that we may sit
Closest to You from right and left.'

And then their master cried out loud,
For this was just a homemade bait:

'You do not know what you have said!
You do not know what you have said!

If only you can drink my cup,
And are able to bear my name!

But sitting on my right hand side,
And sitting on my left hand side

Is not for me to give to you,
But those for whom they are prepared.'

And when conspiracy breaks loose,
There is despair and hopelessness.

The Master then called up His men
Upon the gates of Jericho

To come to Him and lend their ears,
And said to them as He would do,

That whoever wanted His throne
Should be a slave to all the men;

That whoever wanted to lead
Shall come, at last, to be the led,

For men are kings, not to be served,
But should be kings, that they may serve

And give their heads to be the price
For all the children in the dumps.

A blind man would later be called
To serve as did the Son of Man,

That men can see and learn to serve,
Long after He has gone on brake.
(2010)

(19) The black star

He led a life of no value,
And when his eyes were raised at us,
He saw it all but not his kin.
Sending himself to demise flash,
He vowed to quit, but not alone.
As he set out to accomplish,
He took with him Great Fortitude,
And left no escape plan on guard.
When execution let him down
And threw him straight into the hands –
The waiting hands of our agents,
To face us from behind the bars,
In his faeces, urine and sweat,
Until our father calls his name,
A god who fails had failed again,
And he will live to see us live.
                        (2009)

(20) The brown pear leaf

In curves of downward stops,
The brown leaf drops from up,
Diving and gliding home
From where it first saw light,
Through contemporaries
With all the shades of green,
To fin'lly gently land
Like ancestors before,
To replenish the crust
To help the trunk to build
A livelihood for us
Of avocado pears.
                (2007)

(21) The tern

He stays so long in maiden flight,
But sees the sky not as his height.

Like waters that would seek to rise
But fall as rain beneath the clouds;

Like 'great masters' who drifted down
To make our home their winter gown,

But yet, at last, did pack their bags,
The tern will fall down to the earth.
(2009)

(22) This can't be true; this can't be true; I can't believe!

As I slowly walked out of the Mfundi High Court,
A thought, overwhelming, fuming with dead anger,
And piercing straight, right into me, then lamented:
'This can't be true; this can't be true; I can't believe!
This can't be fair, by any imagination,
That people eat good food and seep Italian wine,
And sleep in peace at Nkondengui, on all their deeds!
Our women and children are suff'ring and dying,
And those who manage to survive today are slaves –
The hawker-children, grandparents who can't go home.
At all, indeed; at all, indeed; at all, indeed!
The multiple lives with the pleasures of the flesh
Make no sense, for the life we lead comes once for all!'
As suddenly as he had overwhelmed my mind,
As suddenly as he fled me and found his way,
And while I watched him disappear before my eyes,
His first line echoed and re-echoed time again:
'This can't be true; this can't be true; I can't believe!'
(2009)

(23) The silly arse licker

Heaven and earth have posed for us,
And you are all a part of us;

When you receive a jot of salt,
And the old devil, you exalt ...

O you, this silly arse licker!
How will you be an insider?
                    (2012)

SIPHONAPTERA

(24) Siphonaptera: A letter to Dad

They are flat, O Dad!
They are not round,
They cannot help us,
But they take all that is ours.

They are blood fleas
That live to be thirsty
In small wingless bodies,
Hard and laterally compressed.

They are vampires
With legs to leap and stick –
Reanimated creatures
That have once been dead.

They live not like us,
But bore spider holes,
And come up all night
To rule us in our sleep.

They have, as course,
To live while dead,
And suck us dry,
While we sink asleep.

They prey on us,
Like the lady next door,
Who clutches her lover
And drowns him while at sea.

They leap onto us
And stick and pin us down,
To toe the line for them,
Bodies too tough to crush.

So, ours is just to live,
Like the buffalo herd
Grazing at Kilimanjaro,
Who die in shame and pain

As their health determines,
At the hands of the big cats
That roam the slopes,
To keep their kinds.

O how we part
In the vibrancy of our youth
Like old frustrated devotees
With no bequest and patrimony!
                    (2007)

(25) Children in bondage

Too much to bear, too much to bear,
We all can hear the children cry.
On no single passage of day,
Do we not hear them cry aloud.
You must not keep them in your wing!
So, tell us now, for we should know:
When shall you let them go their way,
For they are free, and should be freed?
So, if they are not part of you,
Just let them be with who they are.
              (2008)

(26) Let's no more leave the riverside

I see in our so-called father,
The man who takes away our cloths
Each time we strip to take a bath.

O yes, he takes them once again,
And there he flees towards the woods!

Let's no more leave the riverside;
Here, we can grow peas and tubers
To see us through the interim
Than go on running after him,
What leaves us rather mad children.

That's right; let him go with the clothes
And go right on to put them on,
For he has certainly been cursed.

And we should not mind it at all;
A passer-by will see us here,
All stranded in our nudity,
And will rush down to our rescue,
And we shall dress up once again.

O yes, o yes, o yes, o yes,
The earth will know the day of rain;
When time will come, we all shall dress,
Never to go naked again.

(2012)

(27) I won't accept a sit on top

I won't accept a sit on top
In that prolonged executive
Which no one leaves and continues
In their old ways of doing things,
And yet, can be thrown out at will,
With a simple stroke of a pen,
And freedoms that may be at stake.
Let me be here with all of you,
Where we are safe in our numbers,
And have nowhere to drop down to.
While those dedicated jujus
Can sadly drop from where they are –
A tiny rope on which they dance,
A twine that would give way at will
If they, themselves don't miss a step –
Down to the dumps where they should be,
We cannot drop from where we are –
A platform at the base level
Where we can press our soles right down
And feel the rhythms of the quake
That leads us through the gentle lanes
To where we finally set sail.
                    (2012)

(28) The first major tremor: A second letter to Dad

Rusted pipes of the ancient art,
And shortcomings of the old plumbers;
Maintenance gaps of our time,
And the choice to stay behind the clock;
Leakages of the resulting chaos,
And the gases that build a time bomb.

Then, what looked like a shying lamb
In the cold dew of the rising East
Soon became an enraged killer wale
From the calmness of the silent deep
With gentle breeze of the late Harmattan,
Energy, mustered from a juicy breakfast
And momentum from the word 'go.'

The only thing it takes, so clear to all,
One failing strike of a match stick
To raze a house of losing cooking gas
And at the speed of light, reduce to ash
A peasant farmer's life-time accomplishments;
The slightest lightning fall before Monsoon
To fully set ablaze a dehydrated bush
With all its water sources depleted
By eucalyptus trees that roam the land.

As fate would hold, there was indeed lightning,
And the fire that had started that early morn
Had, in all earnest, been poorly managed,
For, of all the foresters that play the lords,
Not one, at all, could prove a fireman,
Having taken the flashy heavens for granted,
And were never set for such an inferno.

The fire then grew wilder and wilder,
And for four days, it ravaged through
Five of ten main sectors of the forest,
The five that teem with flora and fauna,
From the central core throughout the West,
Carving out the sheepish North, East and South
Where the housefly shares in every meal,
Or game escapes no hungry jaws,
And townships have no linking roads.

Then, something, in earnest, came to pass,
So remarkable in its senselessness:
On the evening of the fourth infernal day,
The captain of the team of foresters
Marched up, in all the airs of His Excellency,
And emptied a whole tanker of super benzene
Into the angry conflagration of blazing rays –
The roaring naming of the folks
And the violent hitting of the desk at them.

Intriguingly, another surprise was up for grasp,
As the unexpected, again, came to pass:
At day-break of the following day,
The unforgiving hellhole solemnly caved in,
Leaving the onlooker with the theory
Of the eminence of an epic come again.

It had all taken the foresters really unawares,
And to every intent and purpose,
Left them gravely mortified and discomfited,
With their ineptitude and bad faith uncovered,
As, under his master's watchful eyes,
The lousy keeper of gold and silver, then revealed
That, alone, the sovereign water-way station

Had suffered a depressing sixteen billion shift.
What much treasure there is in a follicle –
A single hair follicle of a great elephant!
Where is the gold, and why is it not seen?

If it was a jock of the chariot of the gods,
Then it was just the first major tremor,
And a modern Pompey will soon make landfall,
And millions can die in the heat of the game
If the seismographs are not the chosen of the folks.
(2008)

(29) Green bananas won't stay green

I was pilling off the skin of green bananas
To boil them and feed my hunger.
As I broke upon the first green banana,
He suddenly began to change his complexion.
I had wanted green bananas and nothing else,
So I put the one poised to change, in the fridge,
Not to stop him from changing, anyway,
But in order not to expose his mortal wound.
How I also felt that the change won't come!
It was only a couple of days thereafter,
And he was brightly flaxen and swollen,
Grinning and smiling from molar to molar.
So, I suddenly came to the 'Thomas effect'.
Had I even been placed on a mission
To stop the banana from reaching his goal,
Freezing him in a black pot of nitrogen
Would not have done the deed,
And all my efforts would have been futile,
For green bananas won't stay green.
(2009)

CURSE

(30) Curse

We won aloud and won again,
And we have done so once again.
The trophy seems to've come to stay,
And as they gain in number by the day,
The skills of rope dancing ever on the rise,
A glorious promise land now keeps her price
To hold command of the club for years to come
And remains heads up, with no challenge to come.
(2007)

(31) Speak with me!

Isn't there a new language
That we both are fluent in?
If we can utter the words,
We shall build a new nation.
Let us speak, and do so now,
Lest we lose the precious gift
Of the essence of our being,
Much ado about nothing!
                      (2010)

(32) Sir Robert's address: The death craft at the Durban coast

A dead market for resuscitation
And millions of hungry jaws to be fed.
This is Sir Robert's address on this day,
A sit of thorns that knows no sympathy:
A daily scramble at the border lines,
And gentle China helps by way of arms.
So while the world awaits selection scores,
Sir Robert signs a deal to arm his men,
And in the row after the barren poll,
The many stresses of the English men
And anxious barks of a toothless bulldog,
A Chinese death craft for the interior
Is caught fidgeting at the Durban coast
To steal its doom cargo across the land.
On this, the rainbow nation breaks apart,
And as Mbeki is ev'rything but clear,
The masses win the backing of the law,
And with a high court ruling of Durban,
The doomed cargo vessel is turned away.
So, like the hopeless folks at his address,
Sir Robert's bullets leave the Durban shores
To hit the waves again in hopelessness.
(2008)

(33) Leftward movement

A South African has fallen
Into the well that he himself had sunk
To drown the turn takers,
And so, at long last,
The sun has burnt the house.
Though some brand him the best,
The contrast has been with himself,
For no one had come
After Madiba, the legend,
Other than that wanton boy
Who failed to look at Robert's eyes.

O,
How they compare with the future!

To keep your foes in-situ,
You must be there yourself,
For while you stay up in the tree,
A dowel, however good,
Won't do the job for you.
But if you move to the left edge
And really want to hold it firm,
Kindly deliver as many a hug
As are those who need the hugs,
For, hugs will always be required.
                        (2008)

(34) The express mail

I gassed the men, you know so well,
And here across, I now can tell:

I feel no pain, for I am gone;
It seems penal, but little gain
To take my life for what I've done,
When after all, there is no pain

And no remorse outside the door,
When life is gone, and life's no more.
(2007)

(35) At the steering wheel

O comrades of this very noble art,
I know a place where racing is so hard
Or soft a thing to grapple with as art,
Depending on the ward that bears your card.
To reach your destination is a task
In case you place your card in the wrong ward;
At any one stone throw, you have to ask
A secrete squad if you should push forward.
Besides, the highways are all tiny strings
That manoeuvre through shanty neighbourhoods
With broken vehicles that bear broken rings
And break at will, away from neighbourhoods.
    You run over a man at the blind bend,
    Or into broken trucks that spell the end.
                                (2011)

(36) Tolerance

O no! O no! That cannot be.
You are the one to learn from me.

Learn, for example, tolerance,
This thing that keeps you in my glance

Although I'd been before you, here;
It's clear, for sure, I won't be here,

Had you sprung up before I came,
Or else you would have had me tame.
                              (2011)

THE WOODPECKER

(37) The woodpecker

In his ashy gray outfit,
The woodpecker camouflages,
And we can only but spot
A red beret against the trunk,
In a rapid tapping motion
As in a 'kock-kock, kock-kock-kock,'
Like the knocking at the doors,
That is, in fact, right at our home!
And he is always at the doors,
Knocking, 'kock-kock, kock-kock-kock,'
To take away our youths from us.
Unless he can return to his own roots,
We remain forever under siege
With these daily dreadful knocks.
                                (2009)

(38) Power

A plain working daytime,
The rain was falling though,
As I got to the place
Where dons pen down findings.
The parking lawns were there,
And while car parks were free,
Two cars stood at the door –
The entrance to the block
Where many an arts don
Report daily to work.

And when I wondered loud
How rain can be so damn
To rain in such a scene,
An onlooker colleague
Smiled and fondly said:
It's power, don't mind, it's power;
It's power, it's simply power.
                        (2012)

(39) The saga of Sandra Laing

As we cannot sew white cowpea
        And keep the tan,
Our type's holly, and we must be
        To keep the yarn,

For Sandra's saga comes alive,
        As we have sought
To see that no bound'ries survive
        Within our sort.
                (2009)

(40) Come-no-go
(For Isaac)

That late afternoon, at sunset,
As he trod down along the long street
Out of the little town of Buea,
I did recall the little old slang,
'Come-no-go,' he'd said was thrown at him
That early morning, at sunrise,
As he'd trod up along the same street,
Into the same little town – Buea,
By a man, now on his own last legs.
No one has come to stay, anyway!
                    (2012)

(41) And I fear not

And I fear not
      My ship captain
Who takes me through
      The tempestuous waters
Of this passage
      I make, of my own life,

For I step not
      Upon his toes,
But I call him
      And say I'm safe aboard
And hope to shake
      His hand when we arrive.
            (2011)

(42) The lady of July: An epitaph
(For Dad)

How breath is freely bestowed upon us!
And how nice it is to have a lungful!

While we are meant to leave it all behind,
It is but fine to leave it at long last,

As we embark, not just to pull the dust,
But more to justify our time aboard,

So that, in creation, should there not be
A ridicule of its own creator.

Here lies, beneath, the lady of July –
The star that drew onshore all day and night

And drew inland, right far up to her prime,
With her, and from the womb of the great deep,

The brightly dyed coral reeves of her time
That brought us life and full doses of life

In bright and colourful, exciting shades,
But ev'rything, with her, so soon returned

At the hands of a nasty god of doom,
And though we live, for now, we barely breathe.
                    (2006-2011)

(43) The rhythm of my heart

A car pulled up and then stopped
Opposite where there was already one
That had earlier pulled up and stopped,
And the street, a very narrow one,

Was rendered two times much narrower,
The rhythm of my heart, as many times faster.
                    (2012)

(44) O Michael!
(For Mary)

Once more, the rains have come from the blue,
For, although the dark clouds, one could see,
Those clouds were not here, but far away,
And although we have reached November,
This earth's still wet, nasty, and slip'ry,
And the path we tread's still perilous.
O Michael, the flood has borne you far,
And now, once again, the eyes of tears!
Once more, eyes have burst, and tears so ooze.
                      (2012)

DILAPIDATION

(45) A dilapidated basket:
... now ringing the bell softly

We have a woman each;
So, along a frantic hallway
Where policies are made,
A tired radical cautions:
Much is often done about
These many virgins of ours,
As though it were some felony
To salt them away for our boys.
As we close our eyes and pillage,
And refuse to suppress our thirst,
Let there be no tears at full time,
For unless the wind passes by,
A hen's anus, we cannot see.
The winds aren't here yet,
But maybe not far away.
                    (2009)

(46) We humble through the humble gates

With little steps, we cannot spurn the lanes
Unlike the things that be the quiet ends.
We take upon a journey down the drains
Each passing day, through time that never ends,
And ev'ry moment passes through our way
Without retracting till departure dates
And meeting points from where we pass away.
From there, we humble through the humble gates
Into a yard where we shall meet our host
At dusk, to give account of the voyage,
And how each man has manned his given post.
A man, woman, or youth of any age
    Will freely dine and wine on their own sweat,
    And get the bed, their sweat had rendered wet.
               (2010)

(47) Rest: The peace at crest
(For Julie)

O Rest! O come, and let me sleep!
But not before the light goes deep,

Stooping down to the sombre west
And I get not the peace at crest,

For I should toil the world over
And see not my being forever,

But to the end of road, can walk,
And at the humble gate, can talk

To them who will duly walk me
There where I will set out to sea,

And them who will stay back on land
To see the worth of mine own hand.
(2012)

A Letter to Mom
(Cc. Dad)

The rain fell from the blue,
The rain clouds far away,
And I should bear with you
On all that's come my way.

Beloved, you did your bit
And now live on in it.

Immense, I've been by thee,
Whose being has hallowed me.

You taught me how to lead
The life that men should lead,

And how not to betray
Good folks on my pathway;

To ward off transgressions
But live all impressions;

To squash not naked toes,
And abhor not my foes;

To give when I should give,
And know when to receive;

To love those who need love
And have them hand in glove,

To give them potency
To get on through to see

Sunset with excitement,
And charm, and fulfilment,

Griefless farewell speeches
When the full time reaches,

Unlike it was for you,
Just when, out of the blue,

The rain did fail to tell.
In this, your name will sell,

And so by the Most High.
O Mom, when I shall fly!

With tender memories
Of all the sweet stories

And love that left me sad,
All of yours little lad.
(2003-2012)

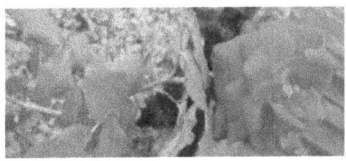

www.ingramcontent.com/pod-product-compliance
Lightning Source LLC
Chambersburg PA
CBHW070325100426
42743CB00011B/2556